# *Pocket Monologues for Women*

Susan Pomerance

Dramaline Publications
36-851 Palm View Road, Rancho Mirage, CA 92270

**Library of Congress Cataloging-in-Publication Data**
Pomerance, Susan.
    Pocket Monoloues for Women / Susan Pomerance.
        p.  cm.
    ISBN 0-940669-36-6  (alk. paper)
    1. Monologues. 2. Acting. 3. Women—Drama. I. Title.
PN2080.P664  1997
812'.54—dc21                                        97-24251

Cover art by John Sabel

This book is printed on 55# Glatfelter acid-free paper, a paper that meets the requirements of the American Standard of Permanence of paper for printed library material.

# CONTENTS

**DRAMA:**

## COMEDY:

# DRAMA

# REBECCA

*Having experienced the death of her mother, and the serious injury of her father, Rebecca is vehemently opposed to drunk drivers. In this scene, she refuses to give her date, who has had too much to drink, the keys to his car.*

Stay away from me, I said! (*beat*) No! You're not getting the keys. There's no goddamn way on Earth you're getting these keys, so forget it. Either I drive you home, or you say here all night. (*beat*) Stay back, dammit! (*beat*) Bullshit you're not drunk. Look at you, you can't even stand up, for God's sake. You're bombed. (*beat*) I don't give a goddamn if it *is* your car. It may be your car, but it's someone else's life.

Do you realize that part of my future was taken away by some drunken son of a bitch like you? Some irresponsible, thoughtless, drunken son of a bitch? I had a mother once, and a father who used to be able to walk. But all of that was taken away in a flash because some drunken bastard, some macho fool, had to prove he wasn't loaded. (*beat*) Oh, really? Well, let's hope, God forbid, let's hope you never have to go through it; have to hear the doctor tell you your mother's dead and they're working on you father.

Let's hope you never have to sit and wait through minutes that seem like days while they try to save the life of someone you love.

(*beat*) Shut up! Shut up and listen!

Today, in a condo across town, there's a man, my father, who lives alone in physical and mental agony because some drunken bastard crossed the center divider. In one single second his life was altered forever. I've seen what it's done to him, I've seen his pain and anguish and sense of loss, I've see a home that used to be full of love and joy turned into empty rooms. And every day he relives the moment. Every day he deals with the part of him that was taken away. We both do.

I don't allow myself to imagine the future very much, because part of my future was removed in a second out on the interstate. Since that night I don't assume that things are going to happen the way I want them to. My future is the moment because I'm scared to death to look forward, to have too much hope.

The bastard who hit us is doing fifteen years without parole. This is some satisfaction, a little. But it'll never bring back my mother or restore my dad, it'll never fill the emptiness in our lives. When someone you love is taken tragically, part of you goes with them. In a way, part of you dies, too.

So, you're not getting these keys. I either drive you home, you stay here, I call a cab, or I call the cops. You figure it out. Anyway you want to slice it, you're not driving, understand? And, after tonight, you're not seeing me.

# DORIS

*Doris expresses the plight of those whose lives are shattered by the devastation of flooding. It is a plangent wail heard often by the families living in the low-lying areas near the mighty Ohio and its contiguous streams. But, even though the ruin is heartwrenching, she is determined to overcome, return to her property, rebuild, and get on with living.*

When we got the word from the National Weather Service, we knew it was gonna be bad, we knew we was in for trouble. We heard the warnings and how people were bein' forced outta their homes up-river. Over five hundred homes in Ashland was under water and people were sleepin' at the Armory. So, we expected it was gonna be a mess.

We got the word to clear out late in the afternoon. They said that the river was gonna crest sixteen feet above flood stage. There wasn't any time to take stuff. We just grabbed up a few things and lit out in the pickup. I looked back at our place as we drove off, tryin' not to think the worst.

The water came in high on Wednesday, rollin' down on us like thunder. You could actually hear it comin' on, bringin' with it people's past and future,

6

their hopes and dreams. You could hear the crackin' and rippin' and bendin' as it came rollin' on down. The old Ohio was a-talkin' to us, and what it had to say wasn't good.

When we arrived at the high school, half the town was there. The Red Cross had set up cots and was handin' out blankets. They had some fast food and hot coffee. People was a-millin' around like they was lost, not speakin', just bein' silent, knowin' that the river was beginnin' to sweep away their lives. One tall, thin little girl was a-walkin' around in a daze in the middle of the gym, holdin' an old, brown-streaked, stuffed monkey tight to her chest. It was all she had. That and the clothes on her back.

We had to stay holed up in the gym for two days, until the river crested and was startin' to recede. We watched a little TV they had set up for us and saw what was goin' on on the news, saw the pictures of what used to be our lives. The river had spread out over its banks like a big, ugly, brown hand. Homes was washed away like they was paper goin' down a gutter, cars were turned inta wads of tin in minutes, poles and fences and trees were picked up and taken for a ride to nowhere. Ya never seen anything like it.

By Saturday, the river was down and they let us go on back home. When Earl and I drove up the lane to our place, there was nothin' at the end—nothin'. No house, no garage—nothin'. All that was left was this big, ugly, muddy scar where everything we had had been ripped up and taken away by the Ohio. That ole river just don't like people, I guess.

The only piece of memory I could find was a busted picture of my dad taken back in 1944. Somehow that mean ole river had forgot to take it along. All I could do was sit down and cry till my face hurt. I cried so hard, my tears coulda started up another flood.

But that was yesterday, and a person's gotta move on. You've gotta put tragedy behind you just as fast as you can. I guess maybe this is a lesson a person learns from the river—you gotta keep on rollin'.

# IDA

*After two years in a bad relationship, Ida finally awakened and extricated herself. Here she speaks of the dissolution and wisely acknowledges that men of an abusive nature seldom change.*

It's over. The whole goddamned thing is finished. Enough. After two years of taking his shit, enduring his insults, being domineered, groveling—I'd had it. There's a limit to how long you can try to make a situation work. There's a limit to how long you can swallow your unhappiness. After a while, your emotions erupt. Either that or you become an early basket case, filled with enough anger to sink the Navy.

When we married, Joe was loving, kind, understanding. Then, after a few months, his true personality emerged, and I realized that he was basically a brutish, sullen bastard who hated women. I don't know why I didn't see this before. I was blinded by love, I guess. Jesus, how trite. "Blinded by love." Maybe I'm an idealistic idiot. Anyway, I'd never seen this side of him before, or if I had I'd refused to recognize it. Who knows? Hell, I've analyzed the thing to death, and the more I try to reason it out, the more confused I get, the more convoluted the problem becomes. I've come to the conclusion that you can't really, rationally, unscramble these things, you have to go with your gut. And my gut told me to bail the hell out.

When I told him, he went ballistic. He couldn't believe I was leaving, couldn't understand why. He didn't have a clue. Apparently he was oblivious to all of the insults and rudeness and profanity. Apparently he was either very forgetful, ignorant, or just one insensitive son of a bitch, or all of the above. Whatever, he didn't get it. He said he felt betrayed. *He* felt betrayed? How the hell did he think I felt? I go into a marriage with decent guy, and two months later I wake up sleeping next to Godzilla.

He went through all of the numbers. You know, anger, ranting, disbelief, denial . . . all of that. I just stood back and listened. I wasn't buying. Then he goes into his Poor-Pitiful-Pearl bullshit act. He's contrite. He's sorry. He's under a lot of pressure at work. There are financial problems. The bastard blames it on everything from a sleeping disorder to potty training. Then he moves into his ignorant act. He doesn't know what made him do it. How could he have been so blind? He didn't realize. Next comes the begging. He'll change. It'll never happen again. He

10

needs another chance. Please don't leave. He can't live without me. His world will go to hell.

Well, if I've learned anything, it's that people don't change, not really—they modify. They learn to knock off the sharp edges, but the basic person is still trapped in the mold. It's, like, this thing that defines their personality is always dormant, waiting to pop to the surface. And who needs that?

So I put an end to it. I stepped on it like you do a beetle before it squirms out from under your shoe. Because I knew if I weakened I'd be right back to a fucked-up life, living with a man with the personality of a hand grenade. So I told him to shove it.

I haven't seen or spoken to him in a year. But I get reports. He's living with a girl who's a personal trainer at World Gym. I understand from a friend who saw her last week that she had a black eye.

She didn't get it from pushups.

# MILLIE

*Her father, a once vital presence, succumbed during heart-bypass surgery. Left in a state of suspended grief, Millie agonizes over his premature death, and rails against an "unjust" God.*

He was only fifty-seven years old. Fifty-seven years old! It's so goddamned unfair. He was so vital, so alive, so full of the future. When mother called about his operation, I was concerned, but not alarmed. After all, he was always so full of energy, so healthy. He always seemed . . . seemed so invincible.

I spoke with him on the phone the night before the operation. I asked him if he wanted me to come home. He . . . hell, I should have gone, I should have been there. It was stupid of me. But he was so damned reassuring, so confident and upbeat. He said it was nothing. Nothing but a simple, single bypass. His doctor did two a day. And mother was confident, too. It all seemed so matter-of-fact, so safe. Today they make it sound like nothing more than a dental checkup.

During the procedure, they encountered four blockages. Then his kidneys failed. It was hopeless. He never regained consciousness. Hell . . . I should have been there. I should have *been* there. And the doctors, the doctors . . . those fucking, overpaid, unfeeling bastards. Didn't they know, didn't they have a clue? They have to open him up to discover the severity of his condition?

After the funeral, I went to see the surgeon. He was a pompous son of a bitch; smug and guarded and condescending. And I couldn't help but explode when he said that these things happen. These things happen? Yes, they happen all right, and someone you love is dead. When he laid this feeble cliché on me, I lost it, I blew. I told the cold-turkey son of a bitch that he, like too many in his goddamned profession, were killing people with their so-called professionalism, with their fucking technological dependence. The whole fucking medical profession has become a pile unadulterated horseshit, dedicated to passing the buck.

I spent a few days with mother. The house that used to be so warm and full of love was now cold. We sat and talked and reflected and wept. Dad's presence was everywhere. The things he used to touch, the chair he occupied, his books; every aspect of his existence magnified our loneliness.

We rearranged the furniture. We thought this might help erase memories. Then we went though his closet. Touching his clothing was like putting my hand into his soul. He came into me through my fingertips. Touching his old tweed coat, I could see and hear him and smell his sweet masculinity. And in the pocket of his blazer, I found two yellowed ticket stubs to a movie we'd seen together when I was just a kid. He'd obviously kept them as a reminder of our time together. I was touched, I . . . it's hard to talk about.

Damn it, I should have *been* here.

# DIANE

*As a child, Diane didn't have the advantages of most girls her age. This was because her father had ambled off one snowy Christmas eve, never to return to run his drugstore, or lend his filial attention to the raising of his six children. As a result, Diane had had to work throughout most of her childhood and teens. Here, wearing a look of wistful melancholy, she recalls her past.*

I really didn't have much of childhood. None of us did. My brothers or sisters. We all had to pitch in and help out because mother was forced to take a job as a sales clerk at Dean's Department Store. She was in notions. She was a beautiful woman when Dad left, but him walking off got to her and she went downhill. Not physically, but in spirit, you know.

I never ever knew Dad, not really. He was enigmatic. Not much of a talker. He'd come home from the drugstore late and have dinner and then watch TV till all hours. I don't think Mother ever really knew him either. But she loved him, and doted on him, and bragged on him, and made him feel special. I think he needed that, because I don't think he felt very special at all. Looking back, I think he was terribly confused, mixed up, and unhappy. Of course, he had access to drugs.

After he left, his partner discovered he'd been taking lots of drugs from the store. That's the reason there wasn't much left of his share of the business— what he'd taken was deducted when the lawyers settled up. Thousands. I suppose he was selling it, too. He couldn't have been taking that much himself. Even though he was spaced most of the time. Or acted spaced. Or something. Who knows?

The first time I experienced sex was with Mr. Wendel at the dry-cleaning shop. One night, after closing, we were there, just the two of us. He forced himself on me, fondling me and removing my clothing. Before I knew it, I was on a table between the steam presses. It was all so sudden, so unexpected and overwhelming. Maybe I encouraged him. I don't know. I don't remember. But it happened.

While he was on me I did my best to divert my mind, like you do when you're experiencing pain and try to block it mentally, subdue it, pretend it isn't there. The TV was going and "Gunsmoke" was on. I fantasized what was happening was part of the program, not transpiring in the present. It helped. What was happening wasn't really happening to me, no, not at all—it was happening to Miss Kitty.

# JUDY

*Employed as a cashier at an upscale auto dealership, Judy encounters all kinds. It is a particularly stressful job. Judy, no shrinking violet, expresses her frustrations and outright contempt for the behavior of many customers.*

Fucking assholes! They come in here with their fucking Lexuses like they were bringing in their first-born child, when all it is is a glorified piece of Japanese shit. As opposed to a glorified piece of American shit. When you break it down, it's all fucking metal and bolts and wiring—that's all it is. It ain't human, for crisesakes. But the shit I have to put up with from some of these assholes is unbelievable. Hold on, I gotta call. (*She answers the phone*). Williams' Lexus. . . Mrs. Davis? Let me check. (*She runs her finger down a scheduling chart, then back into the phone*) No, the car isn't up yet . . . No. . . After four o'clock. I'm sorry, that's when it was promised . . . Look, I can't help it if your daughter's ballet class is at two thirty, the car won't be ready till after four. Yes . . . Well . . . I'll transfer you to your service manager. (*She hits the intercom*) Ralph Lester, line three. (*She hangs up the phone*)

There you have a typical example of what I'm talking about. Some rich bitch in Ridgewood with this pressing problem that her daughter, who probably weighs three hundred pounds on a good day, is gonna miss making a fool of herself in a tutu. And she's demanding and rude and a fucking asshole. The car was promised after four. It's on the fucking work order. But nooooooo, she's gotta call up at one like it's got to be three hours early because she's got a pressing engagement she knew damn well about when she brought the fucking car in.

I get me this butthead yesterday, comes in with an attitude, right? He looks like attitude. You can always tell. Guys with sunglasses pushed back in their hair are attitude on wheels. They got this demanding thing, this executive control thing. Control is their life. They fuck over their employees, parking lot attendants, people like me, their wives, their kids. These men who don't talk to their wives, they "take meetings." Anyway, when I hand him the bill, he goes fucking grape juice. "What's this charge?" "What's that charge?". "How come it's more than the estimate?" He's unreasonable altogether. I can't explain, and when I try I get interrupted by his cellular phone calls. I'd like to take the bill and shove it up his fucking ego, but, hey, like I gotta stay cool because I've got my landlord and several department stores depending on me. After twenty minutes of trying to reason with this shithead, I turn him over to the G.M., who has more ulcers than I do.

(*She answers phone again*) Williams' Lexus . . . Yes . . . When? . . . Yesterday? . . . Gimme a minute. (*She puts the caller on hold*) Some asshole with a question about the bill. (*she leafs through a stack of bills, locates the one in question, resumes the phone call*) Yes, here it is . . . The wiper blades? . . . You were overcharged? . . . The price is $16.95, including installation . . . What? . . . You were billed $25.95? Miss, this is news to me. I've been here for four years, and the price has always been $16.95 . . . I think you're looking at the line below, the charge for the license plate bracket—$25.95 . . . Right . . . Thanks for calling. (*She hangs up*) Here's a bitch who pays sixty grand for a car who comes screaming about twenty-five bucks. Happens every day.

When I worked for Henderson's Used Cars over on Olive, the people who came in were reasonable. We didn't sell anything over three thousand dollars— rebuilt junk, old repos, basic transportation. The customers, for the most part, were working stiffs who needed wheels. No bitching, no complaints, no big fucking deal. Here, we sell sixty-thousand-dollar

Swiss watches to people with more money than brains, and it's nothing but one fucking asshole after another.

It's to the point where I can tell you all about a person from the car they drive. With BMWs you get assholes, with arusted-out Pacers you get smiles.

# HEIDI

*When just a child, Heidi was abandoned by her mother, leaving her frightened and alone. Here she describes her early trauma, and her reunion with her mother, who was a victim of schizophrenia.*

I was just a child—five years old. Mother and I had gone to the neighborhood park, as we often did. I loved the park, the swings, the slides, particularly the jungle gym. I was given free reign. It was a lovely spring day and mother seemed happy. There was no indication that she was suffering from severe schizophrenia.

Mother usually sat at nearby picnic table, reading a magazine while I played. After tumbling through the jungle gym, I wandered back to the table, but mother wasn't there, she'd vanished. I'll never forget the panic I felt. My heart turned to stone. The park became an abstract place of a million horrors. Finally, a nice woman rescued me and took me to the police and I was taken to my grandmother's. My father had been killed in Korea.

I was raised by my grandmother, who was very strict and unloving. She was iron. It was as though she was retaliating for being stuck with me. I never felt close to her because she never expressed warmth. And when I'd ask about my mother, I was told to put it out of my mind. There was never any reassurance. So, I grew up feeling confused and lonely and abandoned.

In my teens, it was no longer possible for my grandmother to ignore my questions about my mother. I was relentless. I wouldn't be denied. So, finally, I was told the truth: Mother had suffered a schizophrenic lapse that day, and had been in and out of mental institutions ever since.

My visit to the hospital was a wake-up call to reality. I'd never experienced such a place. I wasn't prepared for the cold sterility of an institution. Mother was in a ward with several other patients. She had aged, of course, but, in spite of it, she was still a pretty woman. It was a touching reunion, and for the first time in years I felt complete, connected, and loved. It was beautiful. We talked for hours, learning about each other, sharing stories that filled in the gaps of the lost time between us. When I left, I was walking on dreams.

When I returned the following week, she wasn't there. She had wandered off again to her alternative life on the streets. There as nothing legally they could do to hold her. When I finally found her, she was

22

living behind the bus station downtown. She was filthy, reeking of alcohol, digging for food in a dumpster. Seeing her like that . . . it was the most devastating, heart-wrenching moment of my life.

She was belligerent and resistant, but my love for her was so great . . . there was no way on Earth I was going to let her sickness keep us apart any longer. I convinced her to return to the hospital. I visited her daily, and slowly her illness became manageable. I think our connection is the thing that gave her the will to beat back her demons. And, finally, she was able to move in with grandmother and me.

She's living with me and my husband now, has been for years. And she's simply wonderful. Vibrant, alive, as I remember her as a child. Thank God my persistence paid off . . . I think it saved her life. I know, without question, that it certainly saved mine.

# SANDRA

*As a child, Sandra was molested by her father. This
has left horrendous emotional scars. Here, in a tense
scene between her and her husband, she attempts to
once again explain how her past has had deleterious
effects upon her sexuality.*

You knew from the first there were going to be problems. We discussed it to death. And now, here we
are, rehashing the same damned issue for the
umpteenth time. You know I've got hang-ups, you
know this, goddammit. So why push me on the
subject? Give me some breathing room here, okay?
(*beat*) What? (*beat*) Don't say, "Nothing." (*beat*) Say
what's on your mind, dammit. If there's one thing I
can't stand, it's air that's not cleared. (*beat*) I'm
sorry, I'm sorry, okay? And, frankly, I'm sick and
tired of saying, "I'm sorry". And I'm sick to death
with repeatedly having to explain. You know the
facts. You knew from the beginning. And it was
agreed you'd give me time to work through the
problem. Now, because I'm not a raving sex machine,
you get bent out of shape.

With my background, it's a wonder I can stomach
sex at all. After my father, that son of a bitch, after

what he did, it's a wonder I can stand the thought of it. And sometimes, to be brutally honest, when I think about you touching me I want to vomit. (*beat*) All right, it's a helluva thing to say, but it's honest. What you want, some sugar-coated reason for my reluctance to have you shove your prick in me? (*beat*) How else do you want me to express it? Do you ever stop to think that a woman's not a sperm receptacle every time a man gets a hard-on? And, in my case, this is even more of a problem.

Night after night for years my father came into my room late at night and lifted my bed covers and fondled me, touched me, ran his hands over my body. Night after horrible night, I lay waiting in fear, knowing that he was going to handle me and enter me and use me like a whore. It was a dirty secret that I was afraid to tell, not only because I was ashamed, but because I was scared to death of what he'd do if I did. While he was fucking me he'd say, "This is our secret. Don't tell anyone. If you do, you'll be sorry." Do you have any idea what this does to a child? To begin with, their emotions are very fragile things, easily damaged, easily corrupted. This is the unforgivable thing. That anyone can sexually invade the sanctity of childhood emotions. It's unthinkable, but, unfortunately, a reality that's exposed more each day.

And to think that my father, a minister. . . . And to this day he feels no guilt. This is the worst of it. It's as though he had divine permission to ruin my life. The rotten, despicable bastard.

And you. What the hell is it with you? If you really loved me, you'd back off, and give me time, give me time to heal without beating me up for not always being sexually compliant. For Christ's sake, Ralph, don't become my father.

# TARA

*Tara and her sister, Karen, had been returning from a baby shower when a drunken driver crossed the divider and crashed headlong into Tara's van. Karen was killed instantly. The moment, suspended in time for Tara, is nearly too painful to recall.*

We'd left the shower a little after ten o'clock. It had been a wonderful evening full of friends and laughter. I usually take the surface streets, but this night, for some reason or other, I decided to take the freeway.

We were moving along when, suddenly, like lightning, a car hurdles the divider and goes airborne. It collided with the front of the van in an explosion of steel and glass. It was so sudden, so . . . there wasn't time to react. There wasn't a damn thing I could do.

I woke up in the hospital with a circle of eyes peering down at me. It was the eeriest feeling—otherworldly. I was in ER and they were busy cutting my clothing away. There wasn't any pain, as I recall, just a general numbness and a slight stinging in my legs.

Later, when I awoke in recovery, my husband, Bob, was there, and my dad, and the surgeon. I was told that I'd suffered a compound fracture of the right femur, a shattered patella, plus multiple contusions.

And I was bruised from head to toe, as if someone had taken a hammer to my body. I was still disoriented, in a haze, and now the reality of pain was beginning to seep in.

When I asked about Karen there was this silence. Nothing. Just these strange glances between everybody. I knew from their silence that it was going to be bad. Then Bob told me. Karen had been killed instantly. At that very moment, I didn't react. It all seemed . . . maybe it was the after effects of the anesthetic, I don't know.

When it sunk in I went to pieces. I mean . . . Jesus. Dead? Karen dead? Impossible. She was . . . I loved her . . . my sister. She couldn't be . . . no . . . NO! They had to restrain me. They kept me sedated for days.

It's been well over a year now, but the memory of that night is just as vivid as if it were happening right now. The car coming like a missile, the sound, the screeching of metal—it's being played back every day in living color. And the sense of loss, while manageable, is still . . . hell, I don't know if I'll ever get over it.

And the irresponsible, drunken son of a bitch who hit us is already out of jail and back on the streets. This is the sickening part of it, that someone like this

28

isn't put away forever. He killed my sister! The thought of this bastard, this drunken, out-of-control bastard, driving again is incomprehensible.

I visited Karen's grave yesterday. I go there often. We talk . . . I tell her how much I miss her . . . I remind her of good times, and I cry. She was so young, so full of hope . . . so alive. And it all ended in a drunken second.

# LISA

*After another drive-by shooting, the police have instigated a rigorous crackdown. Lisa has mixed feelings about this. On the one hand, she passionately wants safety and tranquillity to be returned to the neighborhood, on the other she fears an overriding police presence.*

It was a little after three this morning. I'd gotten up to check on the baby. The girl was standing in her front yard (*points*) . . . right over there. Was standing there talking to her friends. First off, they should have all been in bed where they belonged but . . . kids today, parents. . . .

I see this car coming down the block. Going real slow. When it got near the yard it alluva sudden swerved over and then they opened fire. The girl fell like her legs had been knocked out from under her. The other kids screamed. Someone in the car yelled, "Bitch!" The car tore off. People were laughing inside. It was a joke. They'd just killed a person, and it was funny, you know. This is the value they put on life—nothing.

When we first moved in here, it was a nice, quiet neighborhood. You could go out for a walk and not think about it. Then drugs came on the scene, the gangs. Now you don't go out at night anymore. Not with the drive-bys and that. Even in the daytime you get hassled by lookouts and gang members who harass you with attitude and vulgar language. You get terrorized.

This was the third drive-by in the past six months. One boy was shot sitting in his living room. His blood splattered his family. You're not even safe inside your own home anymore. Now this young girl . . . fifteen. A life wasted.

The cops have clamped down good this time. They've got authority to break up groups, pick up anybody connected with a gang. And we have TV crews cruising the area. It's like we're on the news every night. I mean . . . I'm all for cleaning up the place, but I think now we have to watch out for the police going too far. I mean . . . how do you pick out a gang member? I mean . . . just because a kid is bald-headed and wearing baggy clothes doesn't mean he's automatically in a gang, you know. What starts out to be a clean-up operation might just become an excuse for police harassment. You can't pick up people for just standing around.

But we gotta do something. We can't let these gangs continue to terrorize the neighborhood. Hell, just take a look around at this place. Boarded up houses . . . smashed windows . . . gang graffiti all over. And we have kids to raise.

I dunno, maybe this new crackdown will turn out okay, who knows? I wish I had the answer. I wish *somebody* had the answer. Sometimes I think the whole damn country's going down the drain. You gotta be worried. I mean . . . I want my children to have a life.

# NANCY

*A former singer with a glamour rock band, today Nancy is a real-estate salesperson for an upscale broker. Even though successful, she remembers fondly her days as a struggling musician and expresses regrets for what might have been.*

This is a hard-boiled town. It can bust the balls of the toughest. It's a big-city killer of small-town dreams. People come here looking for the brass ring and wind up with a handful of lead, without hope, their lives shattered by rejection and dishonesty and the reality that only a fucking few persistent, talented, and goddamn lucky ever make it. The town's crawling with 'em. I call 'em the in-between people—writers, musicians, actors, would-be tycoons. They're the limo drivers with screenplays, waitresses with head shots hanging in carwashes.

When I blew in from Des Moines, I was all ego and dreams. I was the lead singer with a glamour rock band. I was "rad." My hair was teased and dyed blonde. My shoes made me as tall as a fucking date palm. I used to parade down the strip looking very androgynous. Didn't have a dime. But I had hopes and that was enough. Looking back on it, when we were sleeping six to a room in some rat-infested practice studio, no telephone—those were happy days. It was all music and landing a record label, and having your face on the cover of the *Rolling Stone*.

Actually, our music was pretty good, and we got hooked up with a manager. But he turns out to be a fucking greaseball crook. I got burned out with eating Pop Tarts, so I got a job at Denny's serving up Grand Slams to senior citizens whose idea of tipping was twenty-five cents. Then the band guys became more interested in getting laid than getting a record deal. That did it. I moved on.

I had this contact from back home with a friend of my uncle's who worked in real estate out here. I took a job as his assistant, running errands and doing his paperwork and setting up showings. He'd give me five percent of his net. It was a pretty cool job and, for the first time, I had a bank account.

One day, while out showing this estate in Beverly Hills, the guy has a massive heart attack and dies and a position opens up, and I talk 'em into letting me take a crack. So far this year I've sold over three million dollars worth of property. And I've got a great place in the Palisades and just went into hock for a new Mercedes. I'm a top producer.

But, you know what? I still would have liked to have made it in music, had a CD on the charts, done a world tour. Then I could sit back when I'm sixty years old and say I made it, I really *did* something. Real estate's been good to me, but as successful as I get, nobody will ever remember me as a star.

# TRACY

*Savagely beaten while on a photographic shoot, Tracy recalls the incident and reflects upon violence in contemporary society.*

I'd gone out on a routine shoot. The paper was doing this piece on spring and wanted some stuff of kids playing, frolicking, you know . . . playing the games kids do when the weather warms up and they can get out of the house after being cooped up all winter. A nothing assignment really, a piece of cake.

So I take a few rolls of film and go to a neighborhood park where I figure kids are gonna be playing, okay? Not a great neighborhood, but, hey, I mean, it's broad daylight, it's my hometown. . . . Like, what can happen, okay? I mean, like, I've shot stuff in flashpoints such as Panama, Haiti, Somalia, you name it. I've been in the middle of crossfire, seen the worst, bloody carnage you can imagine. One of my friends from AP was killed, shot, as he was typing up a story in his van. I've been through it all. So what the hell's gonna happen in my own backyard? Little did I know that my own backyard was as dangerous as the Left Bank.

So I load up and start shooting some stuff of kids playing on swings and slides, horsing around. Nice stuff. Perfect for the piece. No problem. Then, out of the corner of my eye, on the other side of the park, I see a dozen or so guys milling around. Big bastards. I'm savvy enough to know these people aren't interested in fooling around on the jungle gym. When you've been in the tight spots I've been, you get this built-in radar, you know. But I figure, what the hell. I mean, like, this isn't downtown Jerusalem. So I go on shooting.

I'm getting some nice stuff of kids coming down a slide when I suddenly realize I'm surrounded. Then this one guy steps up and asks me what I'm doing. When I tell him, he says, "Sure, bitch." Then this other guy says, "We don't like cameras." I try to explain what I'm doing, but they aren't listening, they're moving in around me, and the kids are taking off in all directions. I don't know why I didn't run either. I guess, after all of the dangerous situations I'd been in, I just couldn't see this as a major problem. I tried being friendly, but they weren't into socializing. Then this guy grabs my camera, and when I put up resistance, he slaps me across the face with the back of his hand. I fell back. I think I was more startled than hurt. He opened the camera and ripped out the

37

film, then smashed the camera against one of the steel poles supporting the swings. Then, the whole gang came at me. I tried to run, but it was too late. The rest I don't remember.

When I came to, I was in Mercy Hospital with a broken jaw, a fractured wrist, and several teeth missing. I had a concussion. My face was swollen beyond belief. The police told me later I'd wandered into a drug neighborhood and that those guys don't want photographers snooping around in their territory. *Their* territory! Why not everyone's territory? Can you believe this shit? I'm being warned not to move around in my own city because of a bunch of no-good, brutal, thieving, fucking bastards who've decided to take over. Here, in *my* hometown.

And I thought Haiti was bad.

# ROSALIND

*Rosalind had the fortitude to walk out on a sick, incestuous situation. Here, in a scene with her brother, she displays integrity when faced with substantial inheritance and considerable family pressures.*

Your call came at me like a fist shattering glass, out of the blue—bam! I hadn't heard from you in years, and now here you are on the phone with that sickening, obsequious voice of yours acting like we'd just spoken yesterday. Alluva sudden you have to talk to me because Dad died and there are questions about inheritance, the mill, stocks. . . . It's amazing how money will generate a call to someone's worst enemy.

It's a wonder the old bastard left me anything. (*beat*) I'll call him anything I want. He was a no good bastard! (*beat*) I can't imagine why he left me a cent. Not after I told him and the rest of you to take your phony respectability and shove it up you collective asses.

And you waited a month to tell me he died. Not that you should have felt any urgent compulsion to notify me. Face it, you didn't give a damn. You all knew what I thought of the evil old bastard who poisoned everything he touched, especially his family, who he used an abused. It's no wonder you're all so damnably fucked up. Not that I'm making excuses for you. You're all weak, greedy bastards who were disgustingly sycophantic in order to get hold of his fortune. You all sat back and accepted his cuts and insults and cruelty and public belittlement. Hell, the son of a bitch drove Mother insane with his constant pressure and carping, and you knew it, and what did you do? Nothing. You all just stood by with your martini faces as she slowly lost her mind. Damn!

The day they hauled her away you all diluted yourselves that her mental illness was some inherited trait. You actually sold yourselves on this rather than face up to the truth: that her husband had driven her mad with his years of profane criticism and public berating. She was a gentle, good-natured soul who lived in constant fear of his tirades and small-mindedness. It was sickening how you allowed her to be put away at Marysville. You weak, self-interested bastards. My own sisters and brothers.

I loved it the way you kissed my ass when I got here. You were all smiles and handshakes. Until the bombshell, that is. Until you found out that Dad had left me everything. Jesus, the look on your faces when his attorney read the will. I'll never forget it. It was priceless. You were completely stunned. You couldn't believe it. It couldn't be. How could he? There must be some mistake. And then, the way you begged and cajoled and pleaded. It wasn't fair. I couldn't keep it all. What about us? Money was dripping from your every pore. If you greedy assholes could have only seen yourselves.

Well I'm not giving up a penny. (*beat*) Oh, really? Well, that's just too fucking bad, isn't it? But none of you are getting your greedy fingers on any of it because I'm giving away. (*beat*) Yes. Read my lips: I'm-giving-it-away!

I called Sam Lambert this morning and told him what to do with the whole bundle—the house, the mill, the stocks . . . all of it. I told him to unload it all at market price and donate everything to Marysville Hospital for a wing to be named after our dear mother. (*beat*) Forget it, it's done, over.

I know you're all going to hate me for this. The only thing you assholes are going to hate more is finding out what it's like to work for a living.

# CARLY

*Up until Carly's entrance into the military academy,*
*it had been exclusively a male domain. Her appear-*
*ance upon the scene was highly disruptive,*
*controversial, a threat to historical precedent and, as*
*a consequence, resulted in her being hazed to the*
*point of personal endangerment. Unable to bear the*
*taunts and abuse, she left after one semester. Here*
*she relates her experience.*

I went in with the best of intentions. My grandfather
and my dad were both career officers, my older
brothers are at West Point. It was, like, family tradition, you know.

I knew from the start it wasn't going to be easy. I
mean . . . being the first woman cadet in an all-male
academy, with their tradition and all. I knew it was
going to be rough. And then, of course, the media
picked up on it, which made it even worse. It was as
though I was under a microscope. But it was
something I really wanted, so I was willing face the
problems.

They never accepted me from day one. It was
either, like, I was invisible, or I was the brunt of all
kinds of jokes and insults. But I made up my mind to

hang in. I made up my mind not to be intimidated. And I think this is what really got to them, the fact that I was not showing fear and cowering before a bunch of tin soldiers. They just couldn't take the thought of a woman showing more strength than them.

But the hazing and harassment got worse as time went on. It was obvious that they weren't going to let up. My being there just threatened the living hell out of them. I'd get stopped for nothing, screamed at, cursed at, called the filthiest names imaginable. I was a slut, a whore a . . . I won't repeat the rest of the language.

Then, one night, three upperclassmen burst into my room and demanded that I stand at attention. Then one of these idiots squirted lighter fluid on my T-shirt and set fire to it. They thought it was a riot. It scared me to death. I mean . . . words are one thing, but physical abuse is another.

When I reported the incident, I was scoffed at. Here three guys set my shirt on fire and I'm told I'm a crybaby. Can you believe it? When I told my parents, they went crazy and demanded answers. They got nothing, nothing but feeble bullshit. And when two of my friends came forward and reported the incident, they were told to keep their mouths shut

43

if they didn't want to lose their Marine Corps commissions. Nice, huh?

The thing with the T-shirt did it. This wasn't just your ordinary hazing, this was over the top. So I dropped out at the end of the semester.

I hope they're satisfied. Now they can go back to training men to become children.

## DONNA

*Since her divorce, Donna has received very little
assistance—moral or financial—from her ex., a
good-for-nothing druggie who has shamelessly
shunned his court imposed responsibilities. In this
scene, Donna, fed up with his cavalier attitude and
neglect of filial duties, unloads on him in no
uncertain terms.*

Now . . . hold on just a damned here a minute,
asshole! Just who the hell do you think you are? Just
who hell do you think you're talking to?

(*beat*) Yes, you. Who the hell else do you think
I'm talking to? I don't see any other asshole in the
room.

(*beat*) Too bad. Too damned bad. Oh, my
language is offensive is it? Well . . . I'm so sorry, you
poor, delicate bastard. Besides, t' hell with the
language,. Forget about the language. It's what I have
to say that's important.

(*beat*) No you don't. Forget it, man. You don't
have any say. You don't have shit, mister. You're
damned lucky you get to see Kara at all, you
irresponsible, coked-out son of a bitch. If I take you
back to court, and I tell the judge what a fucking
deadbeat you are, you won't be allowed within a

hundred miles of her. So don't give me any shit here, okay?

You come waltzing in here, three hours late for her birthday, looking like hell, fucked up. Look, I put up with enough of this shit when we were married, but I don't have to put up with it anymore. You're out, you're history. You should be goddamned thankful I let you see her at all. And you didn't even bring a gift. Not even a gift, you worthless son of a bitch. What happened, you blow it on one of your bimbos, or did it go up your nose?

(*beat*) That's right, leave. Isn't this always your thing? You've run out all of your wasted lifetime.

(*beat*) Naw, naw, don't hit me with that shit. The only person you have to blame for your fucked-up life is yourself. Christ, face up to it, man . . . you're a loser. You've always been a loser, a self-centered, shallow, son of a bitch loser who runs from he hard choices and blames your problems on others; your boss, me, your family . . . you name it.

But—and listen to me good, get what I'm saying into your coke-soaked brain—this is the last time you hurt your daughter. Ever. And you're not missing any more support payments. And you're not coming around here fucked up. Because this is it, mister. This is the end. I'm not buying anymore of your bullshit stories and I'm through cutting you slack.

You pull one more shitty trick, miss one more payment, and the next time Kara will see you is the day she comes to your funeral. Understand?

# MAXINE

*Maxine knows the realities of the mean streets because, due to being physically and sexually abused as a child, she sought independence by becoming a runaway. Even though she is now a successful businesswoman, she can still recall the dangers, pain, and humiliation of her former lifestyle. Here she lays it on the line to a person unsympathetic to the plight of displaced children.*

Then what's society supposed to do, kick them in the dumpster? (*beat*) You don't give a damn? Wonderful. It's good to know that you're an unfeeling asshole. (*beat*) Of course they have a choice. But staying at home where they're beaten up physically and emotionally doesn't give these kids much of an option now, does it?

(*beat*) What do I know? A lot. I was there, I lived it. (*beat*) No, I'm not kidding. (*beat*) I said . . . I'm *not* kidding! I was on the streets for almost three years. (*beat*) Then don't believe it. For three years I was human garbage. (*beat*) Between thirteen and sixteen. My life at home was a disaster. My folks were junkies, and when my father wasn't shooting up, he was either slapping me around or abusing me sexually. I was rebellious and desperate and wanted independence. So, I walked off . . . became a runaway.

(*beat*) Please. No lectures, all right? You're just like most people. You sit back and moralize and pass judgment without knowing what the fuck you're talking about. When you're young and confused and treated like hell at home you do things you wouldn't do otherwise at the age of thirteen.

I was a typical runaway. No money, hungry . . . sleeping behind a warehouse. Then I meet a pimp and he befriended me. He filled my terrible need for an adult who cared. I didn't know enough to be scared. He got me into prostitution. It was hideous. Not only was it totally humiliating, there's the presence of AIDS, tuberculosis, hepatitis, and drugs.

And then, you realize that the person you looked up to as a father figure is nothing but a scumbag user. But here you are . . . trapped. And you don't have a helluva lot of options. Where the hell you going, home? And if you go to a shelter, they don't have enough beds, and the cops treat you like criminals instead of abused children. So, you get in deeper and deeper all the time hoping it's a way out. But it's a goddamn dead-end.

You should have seen some of the kids. Hell, by the time they were sixteen or seventeen they looked like they were in their thirties.

But I lucked out. I was noticed by this woman who worked for this group that helps exploited women and girls. She was kind and understanding and talked me into getting off the streets and into a place called Covenant House. From there, I found decent employment, got an education, worked out my problems and hostilities.

Like I said, I was lucky. (*beat*) Why? Why am I telling you all this? Because a person like you needs to be told, that's why. You need to be told because I've just discovered that you're a hard-nosed person with all the compassion of an oyster. You need this. But I *don't* need you!

# COMEDY

# CHRISTIE

*Christie and her husband have moved from Cleveland to Palm Springs in order to escape the severe Midwestern winters. The intense heat, however, is too much for Christie. Here, speaking with a friend in Ohio, she tells of her bout with heat exhaustion, and her disappointment with desert living.*

(*into phone*) What am I doing? I'll tell you what I'm doing, I'm standing in the middle of an oven. Never have I felt such heat. (*beat*) I dunno, it's hard to explain. It's, like, you know . . . like when you go to the dry cleaners in the middle of summer but worse, because you're only in the cleaners for a few minutes to pick up your dress. But here it's like you're chained to the steampress twenty-four hours a day. It's miserable. Without AC you wouldn't last an hour, you'd be a raisin. And then we get what the idiots out here like to call "desert breezes." Hell, when I left the hospital last evening, the wind was strong enough to blow over Orson Welles. (*beat*) I know he's dead, Irene, it was a figure of speech. (*beat*) Well, what happened was, I lost a bunch of electrolytes from running in this heat. I should have known better. When you look out and birds are frying on pavement, I guess you should be able to figure out that it's too hot for a person to be jogging.

I was out running, and alluva sudden, I get very light-headed. Next thing I remember, I'm in the back of someone's van. All I can think of is that I've been abducted by a serial rapist whose taking me to some piano crate to try out his new sexual aids. Turns out it's a neighbor who found me lying in the middle of the street like a big mound of Nike roadkill. We're on the way to Eisenhower Medical. (*beat*) What? Of course I was wearing clean underwear!

They rush me into ER and do their number and I wind up it a hallway with a guy who'd been slashed in a knife fight. They pumped me full of liquids by way of IV. When they got in touch with Harold, he rushes right over. It was his big idea for me to start running. He was full of guilt. (*beat*) Right. If I play it right, I think I can get a new Jeep Cherokee out of this.

(*beat*) How does a person know? You come out here, the place is like the Garden of Eden with Ferraris. People look good, they're tanned and beautiful. Until you get up close and see they have skin like Rye Crisp. And you're only here for a few days and a hundred and fifteen isn't so bad. And they tell you it's your dry heat. On the surface it's paradise. But underneath it's sand and rattlesnakes and dried-up retired people driving Lincoln Town Cars; fifty pound people going three miles an hour in two- thousand-pound ocean liners.

Right now, I'm looking at a vacant lot full of tumble weed. I feel like an goddamn extra in *Lawrence of Arabia*. For two cents, I'd move back to Cleveland. By the way, how's the weather? (*beat*) You're expecting a high of ten degrees? (*beat*) On second thought, maybe we'll just beef up the air conditioning.

# JENNIFER

*The high-pressure sales environment of the auto showroom leaves little room for relaxed decision making. After haggling for the better part of an hour, Jennifer finally explodes.*

Look, I came in here for a Toyota Camry, okay? I know the model, I know the color, I know what I want on the damn thing. It's not like you have to sell me anything. I tell the sales guy that I have a very specific budget due to the fact that I make less than native labor working for a man who gives you a hardy handshake for Christmas. You know all the details, and we agree on the car and the price. But this isn't enough. So the salesman brings me in here because you're the finance guy. And what do you do? You try to sell me a bunch of shit I don't want, don't need, and never asked for.

Look, Mr. APR, frankly I don't give a fuck for an alarm system. They're too complicated and, without fail, they always go off when you're on the john at three in the morning. Besides, I've got insurance for that. And I don't want special undercoating. In case you haven't heard, this is Southern California. Rust isn't exactly our biggest problem. Now, if you're pushing drive-by shooting coverage, maybe I'm interested. And what's all this hype about leather? I don't like leather because I hate the thought of sitting on a dead animal. I've got enough guilt already without riding around in seats that go, "Moo." And what's this extended warranty shit? You mean the car's gonna disintegrate before the sixty-thousand-mile guarantee? If this is the case, you should be selling me lemon insurance, or I should be buying a Ford.

I should have known from the first I was gonna get hustled. Just the outfit the salesman was wearing was a tip off. Sorry, I almost forgot, there aren't any salesmen anymore, there are only "sales consultants" and "sales associates." Excuse me for being so insensitive. Like you being a "financial advisor." If I wanted fanatical advise I'd talk with my sister's kid who's saved up eight hundred dollars in quarters out of his allowance, not some slider in a cheap Italian suit and cardboard tassel loafers.

Look, all I want is a standard, four-cylinder Camry. Gray. Standard wheel covers. Standard mohair seats. A basic radio. No special wax. No undercoating. No chrome wheels. No striping. No 100-watts-per-channel surround-sound CD with cassette player. No leather. No sunroof. No leather-wrapped steering wheel. No Lojack. No extended warranty. And I don't want to lease or finance, I wanna pay cash. If you've never heard of cash, it's that funny little green stuff that is actually money.

Got it, asshole?

# LELA

*Due to the fact Lela is currently dating a recognized filmeditor, she was invited to attend the Academy Awards ceremonies. Being a sensible person, the product of small-town upbringing and values, she found the affair little more than an orgy of exhibitionism and self-congratulation. Here she describes the event to a co-worker.*

First off, it seems like what people were wearing was more important than being nominated. "Miz so-and-so is wearing a Valentino. Mr. so-and-so is wearing an Armani." And star after star talks about what they're wearing, forget about the picture.

Like, "What was it like working with the distinguished Shakespearean actor, Sir Adrian Dipshit?"

"Well, he always showed up on the set in a Hugo Boss suit of seven-ounce worsted. He was always so wonderfully understated. And never wrinkled."

"I understand that filming in the Tunisian desert was very challenging."

"Yes, but I was actually quite cool in my Ralph Lauren oatmeal linen suit with matching bone buttons. And my Ferragamo sandals were terrific for the desert nights. Salvatore is *such* a genius."

"Is it true that the rate of exchange was a major problem in Tunisia?"

"Yes, but I was fortunate to have lots of dinar in my chic little black handbag by Givenchy."

It was something. Every last one of the stars mentioned their designer. And this is one of the highlights of the evening. The big question on everyone's lips is, "What are they wearing?"

I understand that they get the clothes free for mentioning the designer's names. Which tells you that your average star is one cheap son of a bitch. Here is someone making fifteen million a picture who can't resist getting a free suit.

Then there were the starlets who showed up with their implants hanging out. Instead of mentioning their designer, they should have credited their plastic surgeons. "My breasts are by Dr. Nathan Schwartz, 555 North Rodeo Drive, Bevelry Hills. Six-thousand dollars. I never know I have them on."

I was really disappointed. I expected more glamour. But nobody was glamorous. Even in their Rykiels and Cerrutis and Armanis they didn't have any class. There wasn't any magic. Hell, I felt as classy as anyone. Even though I was wearing a sixty-dollar dress from Des Moines and carrying a not-so-chic little brown handbag full of old Kleenex.

# ANGELA

*Angela, though discouraged, is not naive to the realities of what it often takes to make it in show biz.*

She came into the audition with heels up to her ass. Sat down right across from me. Her skirt was almost on. Every time she crossed her legs you got a picture of her monkey. Dark and curly and thick. And she knew it. Some bitches love to shoot beaver. And guys always go for it. Hey, what guy with a healthy id is not gonna get a mental boner?

She sat, half-ass leafing though *Waiting for Godot,* acting like she understood it, with this stupid, faked-serious look on her face. Hey, she wouldn't understand the label on a can of peas, believe me. Not that anybody really understands what the fuck Beckett was up to anyhow. That's the reason the play's so goddamn fucking popular, because it's a load of abstract shit that got into college and got analyzed by the corduroy-coat set.

She kept flipping the pages and crossing and uncrossing her legs, exposing her monkey factory. It was a show. It was almost worth the wait for the casting guy, who was already forty minutes late because he was an asshole who liked to keep people waiting. But what am I gonna do, leave? They know you're a struggling piece of shit who'll sell their grandmother for a part, so they treat you like something on the bottom of their shoe. Forget about "compassion" and "art." This is the garbage you hear when you're doing *The Time of Your Life* in high school and pretending to be a rock in college drama. In reality, it's all business and how cheaply they can get you because they pay fifteen fucking million dollars to Tom Cruise.

Between takes on her bunny, I asked her what she was reading for and she said the part of a child psychiatrist. I damned near choked on my spit. This wouldn't miscasting, this would be absurd. But she's convinced she's perfect for the part because she's seen *The Miracle Worker.* When I asked her how she'd gotten into acting, she said that when she was selling popcorn at a Cineplex, Dustin Hoffman told her she had a nice quality and gave her the name of an agent. Hey, when she bent over to put on butter, he probably got an eyeful of the mink stole between her legs.

When I told her I'd studied at the American Academy and had done some off-Broadway, she wasn't impressed. She just swung a leg over and opened me up her world of primitive delights, which caused me to lose my concentration altogether. This bitch could start wars with that thing.

The casting asshole finally showed up and I did my thing. I read for the part of Gina, an intense, twenty-six-year-old, brooding Italian type. And because I'm an intense, twenty-six-year-old, brooding Italian, they told me I wasn't right for the part.

In the parking lot I run into Ms. Bareass. She's getting into a new Corvette and showing off her chimp. She tells me she got the psychiatrist part, that the guy said she was perfect for it. Hey, after one glance at that ten-pound bush between her legs, he would have cast her as Mother Teresa. But, like, you know, I really don't resent it. I have to give her credit for using her endowments. Unfortunately, the only endowment I have is acting ability.

# NICOLE

*Sex is wonderful, but you don't turn it off and on like a phone service. Here Nicole, a worldly, independent woman, makes it abundantly clear that she does not appreciate being used for sexual convenience.*

I don't mind having sex in the morning. What I *do* mind is being woken up for it. It's not like I'm room service. I'm not your 911 sex wake-up call. This isn't the way it works. Usually, when I'm in bed, and my eyes are closed—guess what? I'm sleeping. Surprise, surprise. And when I'm sleeping, my sex system is turned off. It's on hold. It's dormant. It's shut down. Off. In other words, my fuck machine is not running, it's idle. And you don't go jump-starting a cold engine.

As anybody with half a brain knows, you have to let a cold engine warm up before driving. Think of the mechanism between my legs as your car, okay? Do you just go and jump in your cold Mercedes and drive off? Hell no. You let it warm up first. You let the oil get circulating. You're kind, gentle, and considerate. You're Mario Andretti waxing a Ferrari. You're Al Unser Jr. overhauling an engine. You're extra careful not to slam doors. You don't leave cigarette butts in the ashtray. You shake out the floor mats. And in my case, excuse the metaphor, you don't go trying to shove something up the exhaust pipe at four-thirty in the morning.

I appreciate the fact that you're amorous. I like amorous men. They are my favorite kind. Amorousness is one of the prime requisites. Amorousness and money. And, during normal hours, I'm open for business. But I'm not on twenty-four-hour call.

Look at it this way—I'm a private club. I'm discriminating, exclusive, my dues are high, the service is impeccable. But because I'm exclusive, I don't tolerate riffraff coming in at all hours and being disruptive. To these kinds of members I say, "Sorry, membership canceled."

By my Rolex, the time is now four-fifty A.M. And, by my reasoning, right now farmers are crawling out of bed. Factory workers are preparing to start the first shift. The guy who drops off the newspapers is having a second cup of coffee. Night watchmen are about to go off duty. The birds are yawning and stirring in their nests. The guy at the bakery is putting the finishing touches to his second batch of donuts. And me? I'm about to go back to sleep till at least eleven o'clock. And during this wonderfully restful period, I don't want to be interrupted by some inconsiderate son of a bitch whose brain is in his penis.

Goodnight, sweetheart.

# JODIE

*It is difficult for those of provincial background to break free of ingrained mores.*

It all goes back to being from a small town in the Midwest. People in my home town are born old with old ideas and attitudes. And they're very austere and not at all emotional. I never heard my father tell my mother he loved her. His biggest compliment was that she made great pie. "Why, let me tell you something, Edith makes the best pies in Stark County." Apparently her crust was the thing that won his heart. And she wasn't very demonstrative toward him, either. The biggest praise she had for him was that he was a good provider. "Jim's never failed to keep bread on the table," she used to say. I can't imagine them ever having sex. It's just not conceivable. It would be like imagining . . . Edward Asner naked. (*She shivers*)

It's no wonder why I'm so damned shy and re-moved and about as interesting as sweat socks. It's got to do with being brought up in a household where they served bacon and eggs for Christmas dinner, and celebrated all of our birthdays all at one time on May second because this was the day they slaughtered. I still associate my birthday with blood pudding.

I've tried to overcome, but it seems, no matter how hard I try, that my underlying, countrified ways hang on. It's like painting over rust. If you do, it just keeps surfacing. You've got to scrape it all away and start over. And this isn't easy to do when the rust goes all the way to the center of your psyche. Still, way back there in the deepest recesses of my mind are all of these imbedded attitudes and taboos. I still find it hard to buy new things, for instance. I could win the lottery and still feel guilty about treating myself. See this outfit I'm wearing? Well, it's one of two. The other one is brown, too, a favorite "vibrant" color in my family. My mother and aunts always wore brown because it didn't show soil and you saved a fortune in cleaning bills. My dad never owned a blue suit. Blue was "daring" and "showy."

I'm still driving the same old Dodge I bought back home. It's white, because white is easy to keep clean. No one in my hometown ever bought black. Black is impracticable. Black is out of the question. And the Dodge has trunk space. Trunk space is the most important factor when buying a car. Not looks, not performance, not the fact that it's as ugly as compost—trunk space. When my uncle John bought a red MG they refused to let him park it at the family reunion. Foreign cars are out of the question. In my hometown, Toyotas and Hondas aren't discussed in mixed company.

And you wonder why I'm so damned provincial. Why do I wear oxford shoes? Because they're sensible, of course. Brown and sensible. Why do I shudder at the thought of (*She spells it*) S-E-X? Because "nice girls" don't have sex. Back home, women had babies, but they never had sex. Why? Because having sex leads to buying red MGs.

Now you have some insight into why I can't spend the weekend with you. I like you, you're very attractive. You're kind, you're generous, you're considerate. But . . . but the thought of having . . . of being naked . . . of . . . after all, I'm *only* thirty-two years old.

# GINGER

*Ginger has recently become part of the "cholesterol generation," and this has greatly altered her outlook and lifestyle. Once a perfectly normal, positive person, she is now irrationally concerned for her physical well-being. Here she expresses her unhappiness, and questions the rationality of today's cholesterol-obsessed society.*

I was feeling great. Then I make the mistake of going in for a check-up. Of course, my cholesterol is too high. Not by much, but the doctor would like to see it below 200. They always want to see it below 200. It could be 201 and they want to see it below 200. At 200 or below you're perfect, at 201 you're a walking dead person. And at 220, I may only have a week to live. This is how dire they make it sound. "You're cholesterol is 220. Get a will, say goodbye to your friends, do you want to be buried or cremated, would you like donations in lieu of flowers?"

At 220 I feel like a walking heart attack. A month ago, I was having cheeseburgers; today I'm eating sawdust. A month ago I was alive and happy and savoring fat, today I'm wasted and grumpy and gnawing on raw broccoli.

I used to be a happy, carefree person. I was making plans. I was enjoying life. My outlook was positive. Things were rosy and I was eating cheese enchiladas. Then, on the advice of my mother, I go see Dr. Miller and he gives me a check-up, his bill, and a booklet on lifestyle management. Today I'm depressed and irritable. There's no future. My outlook is negative. Things are rotten and I'm eating baked cod fish.

My life is a great big mess of LDLs and triglycerides and lipids and I have this recurring dream of waking up with no eyes, just two big globs of bloodshot fat. You're looking at a cholesterol hypochondriac. I imagine that little, ugly LDL people are having a party in my veins. I can visualize my arteries clogging. I can *hear* them clogging.

Before last month, I never gave a minute's thought to illness and dying. I was a happy couch potato. I just got up and went to work and spent the weekends sucking up pizza. Now, I'm managing my lifestyle. I never thought of myself as a manager. I've never been good with people. Now, I'm managing myself and it isn't easy because I hate authority figures and, therefore, I hate myself. I don't like myself as my manager. I won't let myself eat real food. I force myself to put Nikes in my purse so that I can walk thirty minutes on my lunch hour. I make myself walk up stairs instead of taking the elevator. As a manager I'm an asshole to myself. Nobody should have to take what I'm taking from myself.

I've had it with the lipids and LDLs, the HDLs, the PDQs, the IRS, NBC, ABC, and NATO. I have to live. So I die young, so what? So, it's my business, and the world isn't going to end if I'm 220 with a triple bypass. Besides, as often as I have sex, the scar wouldn't be that important, anyway.

# VALERIE

*Valerie has made the mistake of going home with a
relative stranger. While in his apartment, she has discovered an arsenal of exotic marital aids. Here she
confronts him regarding these bizarre instruments,
and vows to never again impetuously involve herself.*

Do you know what you are? (*beat*) Well, let me tell
you . . . you're one bizarre son of a bitch. (*beat*) Let
me finish here, okay? Any guy who keeps a drawer
full of these kinds of junk is some kind of freak.
Okay, all right . . . a vibrator I can understand. A
nice, harmless little vibrator is one thing, but a drawer
full of mechanized warfare is sick. Who do you
expect to use this junk on, anyway? (*beat*) Sure, sure,
c'mon . . . like, get real. I'm really believing that it
was here when you moved in. Nobody leaves behind
a thousand dollars worth of *Star Wars* dildos.

I guess this is what I deserve for picking up a
stranger. I should know better, I've been around.
When am I going to learn? But you looked like a
nice, harmless guy. And you know my roommate.
But my IQ must have been on serious hold, because
nice, harmless looking guys are always the ones who
turn out to be sickos. It's always the nice, quiet,

harmless guy who winds up with a dozen bodies under his front porch.

"He always seemed like such a nice, quiet person. He was always friendly and never bothered anybody," the neighbors always say. Yeah, right. He never bothered anybody because he was too busy doing amateur pathology in his basement.

Look, you may be the nicest person on Earth, good to your mother, kind to children and pets. You may be active in church work, collect for Goodwill, a Cub Scout leader. But you're also a card-carrying member of the Pornographer's Union. Anybody who shops for sexual aids made by Black & Decker is one weird, kinky person. (*beat*) What? You're last girlfriend bought them? C'mon now. Bullshit! No normal woman would buy these things because she couldn't lift them.

Why don't you just own up to the fact you've got one you can't keep up so you rely on the Energizer Bunny. Instead of an erection, you've got a collection. All of this crap is nothing more than a substitute for your inability to satisfy a woman with the real thing. You think women like plastic? Hey! The only kind of plastic that turns them on is Master Card.

You're typical of a zillion guys who watch too much MTV and masturbate in front of the Internet and think literature is the swimsuit edition of *Sports Illustrated*. You haven't a clue to what being a real man means. And it certainly isn't having a room full screw machines. I'm sure as hell glad I opened this drawer when I did. Otherwise I might have gone to bed with Westinghouse. (*Heading for the exit*) I'm outta here. (*beat*) Oh, by the way . . . do me a favor, okay? Don't ever plug all this stuff in at once. If you do, you'll blow half the power in the city.

# STACY

*Stacy may still be single, but she has her sanity and independence.*

Too many babies, too many children. Babies, babies, kids, children. It's like they're in this fertility contest and everyone's coming in first. I go to their homes and it's wall-to-wall diapers and crying and yucky smells. And they ask, "Stacy, when you gonna get married? Why, you aren't even engaged. What's the matter with you?"

What's the matter with me is that I'm the only one who still has her sanity, the only one without hands that look like I thread pipe for a living, the only one who can still make my car payments, the only one who can take off for the weekend and sleep in and play music loud, and can still afford to shop. I'll tell you what's the matter with me—nothing!

They all hate me for living in a poop-free environment. They hate me for not having stretch marks and broken veins and an eternal bad-hair day. The hate me because I don't have to get up at three in the morning and mop up vomit. They hate me because I'm still able to tuck in my blouse. They hate my freedom. They're a bunch of envious, trapped housewives.

When I go to their homes, it's like entering a war zone. Kinds are screaming and the TVs are blaring and dogs are barking and their husbands, who used to be trim guys in cool clothes, are farting away six-packs in their recliners. Toys are everywhere to the point it's like walking through mine fields. The kitchen floors are sticky and the kitchen cabinets are sticky and the ranges are sticky and there are so many magnets on the refrigerator doors you can't find the godamn handles. Laundry is piled on ironing boards and mountains of unpaid bills are stacked up on back copies of *Woman's Day*. You can't talk, you can't walk, you can't breathe, you can't sit down. Dogs are chewing the hems out of the drapes and cats are coughing up hairballs into peanut butter and jelly sandwiches. The next-door neighbors are always there with their hair in curlers and blood-shot eyes and kids on their hips who are burping up Gerber's. There's talk about pre-school and orthodontists and carpooling and tennis lessons and dance classes and little league and the fact that they're all going broke because they can't afford private schools.

But I'm the freak. I'm the one with the problem. Life is passing me by. I'm not getting any younger.

What is life without a husband and two and three-fifths children, an Old English sheepdog, and a sport-utility vehicle with car seats? They're all sorry for me and worry about me and pity me. I tell them I'm happy, and they tell me that I only *think* I'm happy, that I'm really a miserable, pitiful person who'll wind up old and lonely in a flea-bag nursing home.

I'll admit, it does give a person something to think about. So, this weekend, while I'm on the beach in Cabo, sipping my third champagne cocktail, I may give it some thought.

Like hell.

# JOAN

*She has risen to the apogee of her profession—president and CEO of the world's most powerful entertainment conglomerate. She has succeeded beyond even her most megalomaniacal dreams. Incensed with power, she delivers this heated speech at a corporate meeting. Even though her remarks are bizarre, in them, frighteningly, are seeds of truth.*

Someday soon, it'll be possible to entertain every single person in the entire world simultaneously with one media event. Just think of every man, woman, and child in the entire world sitting down to the same television event brought to them by satellite. Think of it. The Academy Awards is coming close. But we can do better. We can get it all. All! One-hundred-percent-across-the-board viewer participation. Imagine!

All Americans have the inalienable right to entertainment. It's granted to them. "Life, liberty, and the pursuit of happiness." *Happiness.* What do you think this means? It means entertainment. Like the first Thanksgiving. The Indians came and brought corn, right? Well, we're still bringing it, and people still love it because it's basic. It hits them where they live. Basic, solid, corny entertainment that makes 'em laugh and makes 'em cry and stirs 'em up. We've come a long way since the days of the Pilgrims and a bunch of Indians dancing around half-naked to get laughs. Now, today, people have complete freedom from boredom. And why? Because of us, that's why. Because we understand them and love them and want the best for them. And the best is pure entertainment—electronic corn.

And remember—corn is American. Hell, the Indians knew it. Where do you think the word media comes from? It comes from the word "mead": mead—media. And the best media is bright and colorful and loud and immediate and entertaining and unreal. If I'd been content to sit back and keep doing the "real" news and "real" movies and "real" television, where do you think people would be today? Why, the poor devils would be in libraries loading their lungs with the dust of antiquity, at dramas listening to "lofty" bullshit about the plight of the masses, at concerts where not one single instrument is amplified, sitting around reading books. Why, hell, people would be back to incest and the Bible—bored to death.

I realized a long time ago that my destiny, my responsibility, my duty as an American, was to preserve life, liberty, and the pursuit of happiness.

*Happiness!* This is what liberty's all about. What's the point of freedom if you're not happy? People deserve to be happy, and by God, if I have anything to say about it, they're going to be happy whether they like it or not.

# AMY

*We miss you, Fred Astaire.*

Slim, graceful, he moved like a dream,
In hand-tailored suits pinched at the seam.
> A walk like a feather, a song, and a dance,
> He talked with his feet of love and romance,
> Hats, canes, suede English shoes,
> Tapping, singing, but never the blues.
> (*sings*) "Just the way you look tonight. . . ."
Fun.
> Laughter.
> > *Flying down to Rio, The Gay Divorcee.*
All's well that ends well.
> Ginger Rogers in endless spin,
> Gown floating, hair touching the wind.
> > Polished floors. Polished manners.
> > Table linen like fields of snow.
Men in tuxes.
> Women in gowns.
> > Cafe society.
> > > Edward Everett Horton.
> > > Victor Moore,
> > > > Eric Bloor.
Eric Rhodes—"My name is Tonetti,

It rhymes with spaghetti."
Double-entendre and double martinis.
    Sophisticated ladies, too too demure,
    With class, culture, and endles allure.
        Champagne for breakfast.
        Night clubs with little tables and big bands.
    (*sings*) "The way you wear your hat. . . . " Casual
wit.
    Fun.
        Farce.
            Flair.
Cocktail shakers full of frosted elegance.
Limousines longer than days.
        Cigarette holders, silver lamé,
        Women like platinum, all of them gay.
Hats, spats. Cool ladies with hot remarks.
        Kern. Porter. Gershwin. Irving Berlin.
(*sings*) "A fine romance with no kisses. . . ."
Boy meets girl, boy loses girl,
Boy gets girl, and we all get happy.
        Elegant cars, elegant bars,
        Elegant dances under the stars,
        The depressed '30s, but nobody depressed,
        Oh, he was charming, oh, how he dressed,
        A leap, a jump, a flight in mid air,
        Oh, how we miss you, Fred Astaire.

# BETH

*Beth was born and raised and still resides in the Bronx, where she has a good-paying job as a local-haul truck driver, an occupation that suits her aggressive, outgoing nature.*

They all said I couldn't handle the job. Show's that they don't know jack. Most people are brainless. (*She points to her head*) Oatmeal up here, runny eggs. Like my husband. The day I took the job, he wouldn't speak to me. Just got up, ate his ten pounds of fat, and went off to work, pouting like a goddamn baby. He just couldn't accept the fact I was gonna drive a truck for a living. It wasn't "ladylike" he said. When I told him there were plenty of women driving trucks, he said it was because they were tattooed, had pierced navels and were all named Bert. He said I was too small and fragile. I wasn't too small and fragile to do laundry and hang wallpaper and scrub down walls, but I was too delicate to drive a truck. Go figure.

And you should see some of the weird looks I get from some guys when they see me coming in this tank. It threatens the hell out of 'em to see a woman hauling ass. Some of these jerks are still living on the edge of the last century.

This is one helluva job. I'm out there making things happen, ya know. Bringing stuff to people that's important to 'em. Being a driver says something. It says, "Here I am, baby, with a truck load of stuff that makes this country tick." I'm, like, part of the big picture. I saw this sign on the side of a truck once that said, "If you have it, a truck brought it." Think about it.

I'm proud of my job and proud of the way I do it. I can put this baby anyplace I want. Get it as close to a wall as a coat of paint. Over in Queens the other day, I had to back a load of Levi's down an alley to a loading dock. Tight as a virgin. But I blew it in there on the first shot. The guys on the dock couldn't believe it. Said that a week before it took some dude a half hour to squeeze in there. And he had a smaller rig. I amazed the living crap out of 'em. They said they didn't know how I did it without a good coat of Vaseline.

After I'd slipped this baby in there on the first try, they all give me a great big hand. Is this cool, or what? Was like I was some actress who'd done this big scene outta Shakespeare. Only difference, now that I think back on it, is that maybe what I did was better than Shakespeare. I mean like . . . hey, with Shakespeare you don't get Levi's.

# ESTHER

*Although her job is highly anomalous for a woman, Esther is proud of her occupation and the service she provides her clients. Here, over drinks, she speaks of her profession.*

Me? I'm into termites. (*beat*) Yeah, termites. You know, the little things that look like Woody Allen and have gourmet meals on your two-by-fours. (*beat*) Right. I work for Dead On Our Arrival Pest Control. (*beat*) Yeah, I like it. A lot. See this here? This here is my five-year pin—a gold-plated termite. After ten years you get one with ruby eyes. One of the guys has a pin that's dammed near solid gold with emerald eyes and diamond wings. He's been with the company for twenty-five years. He goes back to the days when they still used DDT, before there was any great concern for the workers, the customers, or the environment. He's one of the pioneers, one of the old bug daredevils.

He has some cool stories. He tells this one about the time he got tangled up with a bunch of gophers. They nearly had him for lunch. You get a pack of gophers riled up, my friend, you got big problems. Oh yeah.

Today the methods are real scientific and state-of-the-art. We stress biological and cultural techniques, use pesticides that'll do the least amount of harm. We're especially careful when it comes to pets. You're not careful you got yourself a seven-hundred-dollar poodle belly-up in no time. We had this one dipshit who used the wrong stuff and the customer wound up with wall-to-wall dead cats.

This morning I mouse-proofed a house. The little devils had nearly taken the place over. If you don't control your mice, they'll become as bold as door-to door-salesmen. You let 'em get out of hand and they'll wind up eating meals at your table. The same goes for any vermin. The longer you let 'em go, the harder it is to get rid of 'em. Like house guests. The little creeps get into cracks and crevasses and multiply. Especially fleas. (*beat*) Oh yeah. You let fleas go, mister, you'll have 'em dancing in your shorts.

A pest-control professional has to be ready twenty-four hours a day, seven days a week. Because your pests and vermin have to be hit fast and hard. We're at war with infestation because pests never sleep. You think rats and mice knock off at five o'clock? You kidding? No way. The beady-eyed little rascals are up all night pooping in your rafters.

The main thing is to be thorough. When I leave a location, vermin are at room temperature. Creepy little feet are in the air. Beady little eyes are glazed donuts. I go in straight, I go in hard. Yesterday I did this house over on Snyder Street where termites were holding a convention. When I left—meeting was adjourned.

They call me Miss DOA.

# CLARA

*She is a waitress at the White Front Café, a clean-as-pin eatery just off the interstate. Her occupation has brought her in contact with all kinds, whom, she handles with directness and aplomb. She is a sweet-and-sour, no-nonsense person well equipped to meet life's exigencies.*

(*Wiping counter*) How about some pie, Willard? Just hatched no more than a half hour ago. Warm as a hooker's thighs. (*beat*) Okay, suit yourself.

Boy, did we ever have a strange bunch in here yesterday. They were something, a real piece of work. They came rolling in about half past four on their way to Chicago. Were driving one of those German cars. You know, the kind with a front end that looks like a Barbecue grill. (*beat*) Yeah . . . Mercedes.

Anyway, here they come, parading along with their faces in the sky like possums eating shit. They sat down over there in the corner booth like they owned the goddamned thing, looking around at the place like it was dirty laundry.

You shoulda seen how they were dressed. Holy shit. You know your *Star Trek* movies? Well, this is how they looked; like some kind of far-out aliens. The woman had orange hair and was so skinny she'd be painful to screw. And she had rings on every finger and a diamond stud in her nose. The guys had diamond earrings and one had a pony tail. He looked like . . . well, you know what you see when you look under a pony tail.

When I bring 'em the menu, they ask me all of these stupid questions: "Is your food salt-free?" "You have Perrier?" "Is your milk raw?" "Are your vegetables naturally grown?" "Is the coffee decaf?" When I tell 'em we have regular food like ham on rye and cheeseburgers and fries, they shrink back into the booth like I have bad breath.

After listening to these bullshit questions for ten minutes, I say, "Look . . . what we serve here is everyday food that's loaded with fat and dripping with grease and tastes good because it isn't a bunch of fucked-over plywood. Now do you wanna order or not?" I had more to do than stand around wasting my time with assholes. Besides, most of the people who drive big cars don't tip worth a shit, anyway. So, I go over the menu again: Cheeseburgers, pie, ham on rye, chicken-fried steak, and so on. In other words, we have fat in fat on fat. And guess what? The son of a bitch with the horse hair is either stupid or hard of hearing, because he asks me if we have non-fat bagels. That did it. I tell him, "No, but if we did I'd stick a hot one on your dick." They got pissed and walked out. Thank God. (*She takes coffee pot from urn*)

We get these jerks in here every now and then. I guess this is what happens to people when they watch too much MTV.

More coffee?

# ORDER DIRECT

**MONOLOGUES THEY HAVEN'T HEARD**, Karshner. Speeches for men and women. $8.95.

**MORE MONOLOGUES HAVEN'T HEARD**, Karshner. More living-language speeches. $8.95.

**SCENES THEY HAVEN'T SEEN**, Karshner. Modern scenes for men and women. $7.95.

**FOR WOMEN: MONOLOGUES THEY HAVEN'T HEARD**, Pomerance. $8.95.

**MONOLOGUES for KIDS**, Roddy. 28 speeches for boys and girls. $8.95.

**MORE MONOLOGUES for KIDS**, Roddy. More great speeches for boys and girls. $8.95.

**SCENES for KIDS**, Roddy. 30 scenes for girls and boys. $8.95.

**MONOLOGUES for TEENAGERS**, Karshner. Contemporary teen speeches. $8.95.

**SCENES for TEENAGERS**, Karshner. Scenes for today's teen boys and girls. $7.95.

**HIGH-SCHOOL MONOLOGUES THEY HAVEN'T HEARD**, Karshner. $8.95.

**MONOLOGUES from the CLASSICS**, ed. Karshner. $8.95.

**SHAKESPEARE'S MONOLOGUES THEY HAVEN'T HEARD**, ed. Dotterer. $7.95.

**MONOLOGUES from CHEKHOV**, trans. Cartwright. $8.95.

**MONOLOGUES from GEORGE BERNARD SHAW**, ed. Michaels. $7.95.

**MONOLOGUES from OSCAR WILDE**, ed. Michaels. $7.95.

**WOMAN**, Pomerance. Monologues for actresses. $8.95.

**MODERN SCENES for WOMEN**, Pomerance. Scenes for today's actresses. $7.95.

**MONOLOGUES from MOLIERE**, trans. Dotterer. $9.95.

**SHAKESPEARE'S MONOLOGUES for WOMEN**, ed. Dotterer. $8.95.

**DIALECT MONOLOGUES**, Karshner/Stern. Book and cassette tape. $19.95.

**YOU SAID a MOUTHFUL**, Karshner. Tongue twisters galore. $8.95.

**TEENAGE MOUTH**, Karshner. Modern monologues for young men and women. $8.95.

**SHAKESPEARE'S LADIES**, ed. Dotterer. $7.95.

**BETH HENLEY: MONOLOGUES for WOMEN**, Henley.*Crimes of the Heart*, others. $8.95.

**CITY WOMEN**, Smith. 20 powerful, urban monologues. Great audition pieces. $7.95.

**KIDS' STUFF**, Roddy. 30 great audition pieces for children. $8.95.

**KNAVES, KNIGHTS, and KINGS**, ed. Dotterer. Shakespeare's speeches for men. $8.95.

**DIALECT MONOLOUES, VOL II**, Karshner/Stern. Book and cassette tape. $19.95.

**RED LICORICE**, Tippit. 31 great scene-monologues for preteens. $8.95.

**MODERN MONOLOGUES for MODERN KIDS**, Mauro. $7.95.

**A WOMAN SPEAKS: WOMEN FAMOUS, INFAMOUS and UNKNOWN**, ed. Cosentio.$9.9.5.

**FITTING IN**. Monologues for kids, Mauro. $8.95.

**VOICES**. ed. Cosentino, ed. Speeches from writings of famous women. $9.95.

**FOR WOMEN: MORE MONOS THEY HAVEN'T HEARD**, Pomerance. $8.95.

**NEIL SIMON MONOLOGUES**. From plays of America's foremost playwright. $10.95.

**CLASSIC MOUTH**, ed. Cosentino. Speeches for kids from famous literature. $8.95.

**POCKET MONOLOGUES for WOMEN**, Pomerance. 30 modern speeches. $8.95.

**WHEN KIDS ACHIEVE**, Mauro. Positive monologues for boys and girls. $8.95.

**FOR WOMEN: POCKET MONOLOGUES FROM SHAKESPEARE**, ed. Dotterer. $8.95.

**MONOLOGUES for TEENAGE GIRLS**, Pomerance. $8.95.

**POCKET MONOLOGUES for MEN**, Karshner. $8.95.

**COLD READING and HOW to BE GOOD at IT**, Hoffman. $9.95.

**POCKET MONOS: WORKING-CLASS CHARACTERS for WOMEN**, Pomerance. $8.95.

**MORE MONOLOGUES for TEENAGERS**, Karshner. $8.95.

Send your check or money order (no cash or COD) plus handling charges of $4.00 for the first book and $1.50 for each additional book. California residents add 8.25 % tax. Send your order to: Dramaline Publications, 36-851 Palm View Road, Rancho Mirage, California 92270.